Old Bucksburn, Bankhead and Stoneywood
Patricia Newman

The No. 5 open-topped tram ran from Bankhead to Woodside. The Donside tramway was opened on 8th July 1904. An agreement was reached between suburban and city tram companies to utilise the city tramlines to the boundary and thereafter trams ran on suburban tracks. The first six tramcars were produced by Brush Electrical Engineering Co. of Loughborough and delivered to Aberdeen by rail, arriving in June 1904. In this photograph the tram is going along Oldmeldrum Road in Bucksburn just before St. Machar's Episcopal Church.

Grove Cottage, Mugiemoss Road, in a snowstorm. This was the home of John and Lizzie Ross who had a small farm rearing pigs and poultry. The farmhouse was typical of its type and era with four rooms – two up and two down – with a lean-to scullery and an outside loo adjoining the house. By the time this photograph was taken, a bathroom extension had been added. John and Lizzie started farming after the First World War with Lizzie carrying out the day to day work along with raising seven children. John worked as a granite polisher at Stalker's Yard in Jute Street, Aberdeen. The timber building to the right is the first of a row of chicken houses and there was a piggery at the top of the hill. The trees to the left of the photograph formed a shelter belt and marked the boundary of John and Lizzie's land to the west. The land beyond the trees had a chicken factory built on it by Ross Poultry Ltd (no connection with John and Lizzie). That company was taken over by Grampian Foods in the 1980s. The factory was closed in 2007. All the land is now residential.

© Patricia Newman, 2018
First published in the United Kingdom, 2018,
by Stenlake Publishing Ltd.
www.stenlake.co.uk
ISBN 978-1-84033-800-3

The publishers regret that they cannot supply copies of any pictures featured in this book.

Printed by
Blissetts, Unit 1 Shield Drive,
West Cross Industrial Park, Brentford, TW8 9EX

Acknowledgements

Rosie Nicol, Jen Dalmaine and Lynn Thomas for help and support.
Members at the Bucksburn Community Centre and especially the members at the Beacon Cuppa.
Staff at Aberdeen Library Information Services.
Shona Cruickshank, Jenny Allan, Moyra and Rhona Johnstone, my cousins, for photographs and information.
Andy Milne for his help in identifying the origin of Haudagain
Staff at Stenlake Publishing for continuing help and support.

Further Reading

The books listed below were used by the author during her research. None are available from Stenlake Publishing; please contact your local bookshop, reference library or search for them on the internet. The websites that most frequently sell second hand books are Abebooks, Ebay and Amazon.

The Aberdeen Granite Industry by Tom Donnelly.
Annals of Woodside and Newhills by Patrick Morgan
Brimmond and it Shadow by the Stoneywood Parish Church Literary Guild
Children at School by Margaret Carlaw and Derek Ogston
The Aberdeen Suburban Tramways my M J Mitchell and I A Souter

INTRODUCTION

Bucksburn is in Newhills, an inland parish of Aberdeenshire, in the north east of Scotland. Much of the parish is in what is called The Freedom Lands granted by a grateful King Robert the Bruce to the people of Aberdeen in 1319. The boundaries of the original lands have changed over the years due to purchases and following permission from the Crown to feu land in 1551, but the ancient boundaries are still marked by numbered stones. The income from the land constitutes the Common Good Fund.

Newhills Parish was created in 1663 when it was 'disjoined' from Old Machar Parish. Up until the middle of the 19th century, Bucksburn was known as Auchmull or Auchmill. The first indication of a change of name came with the railways in 1854 when the station at Auchmull was called Buxburn Station. The spelling later changed to Bucksburn.

The principal industries were farming, quarrying and manufacturing. Farming is mostly to the south of Bucksburn and quarrying for granite took place on both sides of the River Don. There were meal and corn mills, snuff and paper mills as well as flax and fulling mills, situated on the burns flowing into the River Don and on the river itself. The farming community benefited from the research and development carried out at Craibstone and at The Rowett.

Bucksburn has now been absorbed by Aberdeen and has expanded with new houses where farmland and mills once stood. There is only one mill left on the Don in this region and the quarries have closed either due to lack of prime granite or declining markets. However, Bucksburn is flourishing and has its own identity and sense of community.

John Ross in his vegetable garden at Grove Cottage. The wall to the left separates the garden from the road. At the back of the garden is a builder's yard. John grew beans, peas, onions, cabbages, carrots and kale on a strict rotation. He is facing where an old cottage used to stand. When it was demolished in the 1950s, the stone was used to patch up the Second World War bomb damage to the north wall of St. Machar's Cathedral in Old Aberdeen. The granite had been weathered over many years and had been dressed in an old manner, probably prior to 1818 when puncheons and chisels replaced picks. This made the stone ideal for use in the centuries old building.

Old Meldrum Road in the 1920s. The tram is a rather battered Aberdeen Suburban Tramways car No. 2 which had started service in 1904 and was by this time at the end of its useful life. The service ceased on 4th June 1927 when Aberdeen Corporation Tramways took over the route. Trams were not only used by passengers; parcels could also be sent and were delivered by young boy messengers employed by the tram company. John Michie, chemist and druggist is on the near right with the traditional sign of the mortar and pestle above. Next is Wilburn Ltd who had a number of grocer shops in Aberdeen and the surrounding area from the 1920s to the 1950s. They carried a large range of groceries – fresh fruit and veg, bread, biscuits and cakes from their bakery in Rennies Wynd, tinned goods and dairy produce. Then there is Bucksburn Post Office with its sign for a public telephone. On the left is the Northern Co-operative Society's various departments. In the distance is the Auchmill Road/Inverurie Road junction with several shops including the Savings Bank and two grocer's shops. Bucksburn Fountain is to the right of the tram.

A view taken from Auchmill Road looking towards Inverurie Road at its junction with Oldmeldrum Road. On the right is John Gray's Universal Supply Stores. In 1920, Gray advertised that he had opened a garage, hiring establishment and repair shop to be known as Bucksburn Garage. He sold Pratt's Motor Spirit and in the photo is getting a delivery. In 1923 he requested permission to store petrol in a tank and to erect roadside pumps. Prior to having tanks and pumps for petrol, it was sold in 2 gallon cans that could be carried on the vehicle's running board. In the middle distance is the corner with Oldmeldrum Road, often referred to as Cruickshank's Corner but at this time, G Anderson, confectioner occupied the shop.

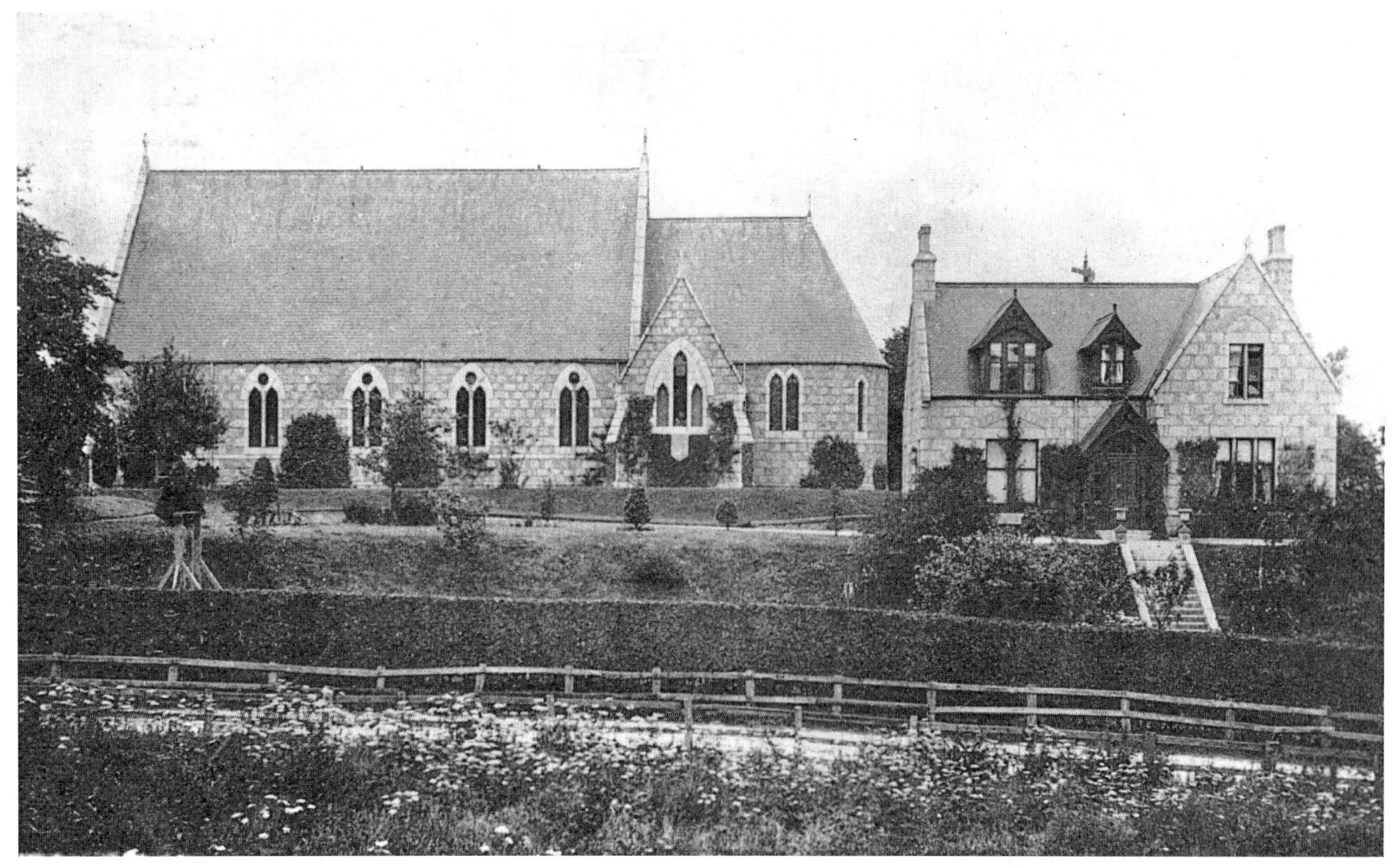

On Oldmeldrum Road is St Machar's Episcopal Church, seen here from Station Road. The congregation was formed in 1874 and the foundation stone of the present church was laid by Bishop Suther in 1879 with the first service taking place on 12th June 1880. The church was designed by Matthews and McKenzie of Aberdeen. The interior is very fine with a superb wooden ceiling and stained glass. R Douglas Strachan provided paintings to decorate the sanctuary. On the right of the photograph is the rectory. St. Machar was of Irish origin and went to Iona with St. Columba later coming to the Aberdeen area to work among the Pictish tribe of the region.

Every August there was a church parade attended by members of the various friendly societies in Bucksburn and the surrounding area. It marched to Newhills Parish Church, headed by the Grandholm Brass Band. All the members of the societies attended in their full regalia.

This is the Grange, still standing in Gilbert Road, Bucksburn. The site was an empty plot when the survey for the Ordnance Survey map was carried out in 1899, so it is reasonable to assume that Dr. Edward Oliphant had the house built. He set up his practice as a general practitioner in October 1898 and lived as a boarder at Lorne Cottage until his marriage in August 1901 when he and his wife moved to the Grange. Dr. Oliphant was the medical officer of Newhills Convalescent Home for 32 years also serving as a civil surgeon during the First World War. He was a native of Banff and graduated from Aberdeen University in 1894. He died at The Grange in 1951 at the age of 84. At the time of its sale in 1956, the Grange had three public rooms and seven

Bucksburn Public School on Inverurie Road. In 1828, prior to the building of this school, a subscription school funded by local people, was built in Bucksburn. The school charged parents a fee for each child attending the classes. The OS map of 1866 shows two schools, one on Oldmeldrum Road near to its junction with Inverurie Road and the other at the top of Mugiemoss Road. The Education Act of 1872 brought in public schooling and as a result, parish, burgh, General Assembly, Free Church and other schools came under the wing of elected school boards. The school seen here on Inverurie Road was demolished when the road was widened. The building incorporated a house for the headmaster.

A photograph of the west end of Bucksburn looking at the backs of the houses on Inverurie Road. The windows of the United Free Church (centre right) distinguish the building from the others. On the far left are the roofs of the school. In the background is the spoil heap of Sclattie Quarry.

This was probably taken from the railway bridge which took Goodhope Road over to Auchmill Road. The goods yard is on the left of the photograph and the main line from Aberdeen through Bucksburn and onwards to Inverness turns off to the right. The Great North of Scotland Railway opened the station on 20th September 1854 when the station was called Buxburn (renamed Bucksburn in 1897). Although the main line is still open, the station was closed for passengers in 1956 and for goods in 1968. The goods line originates at Waterloo Quay in Aberdeen and joins the passenger line at Kittybrewster. On the far left is a 1939 advertisement for soap powder. To the right of the photograph are the houses on Mugiemoss Road. The roof of the Episcopal Church can be seen in the centre distance.

Dancing Cairns Quarry and the Adamant Stone and Paving Company's works stood on the hill above Bucksburn. The paving company was incorporated in 1922 although it had been in existence since 1889. In 1897 it defended its patents in the courts. Adamant produced extremely durable paving slabs utilizing granite waste from the quarry, mixing it with Portland cement and then compressing the mixture into slabs. Seen here is the crushing and screening plant with associated conveyors. Their capacity was 250 tons per day. Many of the slabs had the company's name embossed on the surface and some of these can still be found around Aberdeen today. Granite from Dancing Cairns is light grey speckled. Dancing Cairns was opened in the last quarter of the 18th century although surface stones had been collected for building long before this. Snell, Rennie and May were the first quarry masters. The first newspaper report was of a fatality in 1797 when a spark caused premature ignition of dynamite. A quarrier had his leg blown off and he died of blood loss. Dancing Cairns granite was used extensively on famous structures including Trafalgar Square, Thames Embankment and part of London Bridge. Locally, Thomas Telford's north pier extension in Aberdeen Harbour used Dancing Cairns granite.

Bankhead Road taken from about its junction with Greenburn Road. The church on the right used to be Bankhead or Stoneywood Church, opened in 1879 for the Established Church of Scotland largely to cater for the mill workers living in the area. The adjoining church hall was full to its capacity of 300 in September 1879 when an inaugural lecture was given by the Rev. Mr Skinner of Tarland. His subject was the life and works of Burns. The congregation merged with Bucksburn Church in 1988 and this building now provides office space for local businesses. By the interest being paid to the lorry opposite the church, and also its bulky load, this may be a flitting!

Aberdeen Suburban Tramways ran trams to extend the reach of the Aberdeen electric tramway system to the suburbs of Bieldside on the west of the City and to Bankhead on the north west. This photograph shows an open-topped tram in Bankhead Road on its way from Bankhead to Woodside. It was taken between 1904, when the Woodside route was extended to Bankhead, and 1927 when the extension was closed with the trams terminating at Woodside. The trams were painted red and white. The boy in the middle of the group of three is barefoot so this was probably summertime when boots were not absolutely necessary and poorer families would save on the cost of footwear. The houses on the left are still standing although some of the dormer windows have been modernised.

This photograph was taken from the spoil heap at Sclattie Granite Quarry above Bankhead where the industrial estate now stands. Bankhead is a very old settlement and is noted on a map of 1747-1755. The chimney for Stoneywood Paper Mill is in the distance. The old pan-tiled building at the foot of the spoil heap appears to be the smithy associated with the quarry. In the middle distance to the left is Stoneywood (later Bankhead) Church with houses lining Bankhead Road.

Waterton Road at the west end of Bankhead with Stoneywood Church in the distance. The houses are built of granite in traditional Aberdeen bond and have dormer windows. The cast iron railings were removed during the Second World War allegedly to provide metal for tanks although many were just left in rusting piles. This photograph was taken where the Millhill Brae is today. Telegraph poles were used to carry cables that are now buried underground.

Sclattie Quarries taken from Inverurie Road.

Sclattie Quarry sits above Bankhead and produced light blue grey granite starting in the middle of the 19th century, A and F Manuelle rented both Sclattie and Dancing Cairns Quarries from Malcolm Vivian Hay of Seaton. By the late 19th century, the Manuelles, along with John Fyfe at Kemnay and William Gibb at Rubislaw were the pre-eminent quarrymasters in the area. At its peak in 1896, Sclattie employed 111 men. A and F Manuell also had quarries in Norway, Guernsey, Herm and Alderney. Alexander Jenkins Manuelle and Frederic William Duthie Manuelle were the sons of Charles Manuelle and Mary McLeod Robison. Charles was a Scot, a quarry master and a freeman of the City of London. When Charles died, his wife Mary ran the business for some years until two of her sons, Alexander and Frederic succeeded to it. The area of the quarry is now an industrial estate.

This station was originally called Stoneywood and took mill workers from Aberdeen and from the north of the county to Alex Pirie's Mills at Stoneywood. Trains left Waterloo Station in Aberdeen at 5.30am and at 5.25pm for the day and night shifts. This service started in 1867 and opened to the general public running a suburban service in 1887 until it was decommissioned in 1937. When it was opened for all passengers it was renamed Bankhead. The station stood at the end of Station Road in Bankhead.

THE BOWLING GREEN, BANKHEAD.

A bowling club was opened in July 1909 at Burndale Road, Bankhead, near the railway station. The green did not occupy the complete plot of land so a quoiting court was added. Mrs Lindner, a daughter of the Pirie family of Stoneywood, threw the first jack to open the green and music was supplied by the Stoneywood brass band. The land used for the green was not square so the green could only be played in one direction and, in 1921, the decision was taken to move to a more suitable site. The green and pavilion were handed over to the adjacent tennis club in return for assistance with funding a new and more suitable green. The new green was opened in 1922 at Waterton Road, Stoneywood, and has flourished ever since.

Here are the remaining gable walls of the old Church of Newhills and part of the cemetery. In 1663 the church was endowed by George Davidson of Pettens, just north of Balmedie in Aberdeenshire. Davidson was a great philanthropist endowing many worthy causes, including funding the bridges at Bucksburn and Insch. He also gave the income from the lands of Capelhills (Kepplehills) for the maintenance of the minister and the church. In addition, he gave the income from his lands at Bogfairlie (now Fairley) for the maintenance of St Nicholas in Aberdeen. The Newhills Church in the photograph went out of use when the new church was built in 1830. The prominent white memorial to the left of centre is to Robert Ferries, farmer, of Kirkhill and later of Parkhead of Craibstone who died in 1922.

The former manse of Newhills Parish is now a private house. Originally built in 1771, it was substantially renovated around 1830 by Aberdeen's famous architect, John Smith, who designed the St. Nicholas Kirk screen as well as many manses and country houses. Andrew Currie, minister for the parish from 1918 wrote "I love the old Manse, and I fondle in my heart a wish that the old house in turn will grow to like me, and that somehow it will remember mine and me when we are far from its shelter. For us all comes the day when 'our place shall know us no more".

Kirkhill Cottage lies between the Newhills Cemetery and what was the convalescent home. It was put up to let in 1859 with the attached 20 acres of arable land. Robert Ferries was the farmer in 1891 and is buried in the old churchyard. On the 1905 Valuation Roll, Kirkhill was on the Kepplehills Estate owned by the Rev. James Smith, Minister of Newhills Parish at that time. Kirkhill also marks the boundary of the Freedom Lands. In 1698, "ane great stone, with an sauser and ane Cairn" was noted but is no longer visible. This stone used to stand near the present boundary stone marked ABD 40. The present stone stands against a dry stone dyke field boundary.

The Newhills Convalescent Home was founded by Christian Catherine Smith, the daughter of James Cruickshank, Minister of Stevenston in Ayrshire and the wife of Rev. James Smith, Minister of Newhills. In 1874 Mrs Smith decided that there was a need for a convalescent home for "the benefit of respectable persons in humble life who appear to be failing into dishealth, or are convalescing after non-infectious ailments." At first, she rented Dykeside Cottage on the farm of Derbeth before deciding to have the house above built in 1882. In 1900 the patients included those recovering from tuberculosis. The home became known as a sanatorium in 1902.

The convalescent home, by now much extended was known as Newhills Sanatorium after 1902. In 1903, 73 tuberculosis patients were admitted and 25 were discharged in good health. The purpose of the home was to provide patients with a good diet in a small establishment where they would not be daunted by large wards and long corridors and with access to fresh air. The founder, Mrs. Smith, retired in 1908 after devoting 34 years to the home. It remained as a sanatorium and convalescent home until 1948 when the National Health Service took it over. From 1953 until 1980, it was a home for the elderly until it was sold as a private property.

The road known as Double Hedges runs from the Inverurie Road at Sclattie Park to Eastside of Craibstone. Hope Farm, part of the Seaton Estate is bounded by this road and lies to the south. The Seaton Estate was owned by Forbes of Strathdon until inherited by marriage by Hay of Seaton. The last Laird of Seaton died in 1962. Hope was the first farm in the north of Scotland to introduce a field drainage system in the 1800s.

Forrit Brae runs from the Inverurie Road in Bucksburn to Fairley Road. Until the Aberdeen Western Peripheral Road was built, the road went through to Clash Bog, a favourite walk for local people on a Sunday. It was also the route they took to watch the bonfires on Brimmond and at Clash Bog.

The Clash Bog Well is off to the left of the Forrit Brae or Hope Farm Road. In the Aberdeenshire OS Name Books of 1865-1870 the cot-houses seen above were thatched and in bad repair. At that time they were owned by Mr. Adam of Upper Bucksburn. In this photograph they appear to be roofed in corrugated iron but still in need of maintenance. This cottage and steading no longer exist and the land is now cultivated. Close to the buildings there was a stone well supplied by a spring of fine clear water with a ladle attached to a chain for passing walkers to take a drink. Seen here are two men who are probably drinking from the well. Clash is the gaelic for gully or ravine.

Seen here on Jolly's Howe, which lies near Elrick Hill, is probably Howmoss Croft, a small holding of about five acres on the Seaton Estate. In the 1800s, it was farmed by George Jolly who supplemented his income by labouring at a nearby granite quarry. This pretty howe used to be a favourite spot for picnics and has given its name to a hole on Craibstone Golf Course.

Bonnie Bucksburn Howes.

Howes Road runs from Inverurie Road along the east bank of the Bucks Burn crossing the burn twice before looping round to Northfield. It passes through the area called The Howes or hills around Brimmond which were a great attraction for walkers, cyclists and tourists who would sometimes be taken on a guided tour by Gray and Son of Bucksburn Garage. In 1921 Mackie's Garage at The Corner, Bucksburn were also offering a new Landaulette for hire to visitors. You could contact them by telephone on Bucksburn 6. Local children would go in search of the free autumn harvest of rasps and brambles some of which would survive to be made into jam by their mothers.

At the fourth milestone on the Inverurie Road out of Bucksburn lies the Fourmile Inn with two cottages and a tearoom opposite. Where once there was a quiet country road, there is now a dual carriageway. Although there is a modern ground floor extension, the building is still recognisable. In the survey carried out in 1865-1871 it was a single storey dwelling and public house with a slated roof. The cottages were erected in 1920 by the Seaton Estate using Sclattie granite. They contained four rooms and were priced at £610 each. Julia Wyness Howie, confectioner, lived in one of them and had the tearoom as well. Her name is above the door of the tearoom. She was the daughter of Mr. and Mrs. Howie who had the Four Mile Inn from 1907.

Bucksburn House seen above was described as being 'new' in 1872. The papermaking Davidsons owned the property at one time, but a succession of owners rented it out including the widowed Hon Lady Charlotte Forbes of Craigievar. The pond in front of the house was part of the water management system on the Bucks Burn. The system was designed to control the flow of water to the various mills on the burn. On the Ordnance Survey map of 1867, there were four water-powered mills on the Bucks Burn – three grain mills and a woollen mill. Buxburn Mill, a flour and meal mill near the station in Bucksburn, had a water wheel 22ft by 4ft. A little further upstream from Bucksburn House was another mill built originally in 1616 and restored in 1745. Near Bucksburn House is the farm of Redmyres occupied for many years by the Charles family. Rented from the council, the rent for the farm was halved during the 'hungry thirties' in the great depression when Britain's world trade fell by half and there was mass unemployment.

CRAIBSTONE HOUSE

Craibstone House was destroyed by fire in 1953. Although a date of construction has not been found, it looks to be a Georgian house. At the time of the fire, the North of Scotland College of Agriculture had owned it since 1913. A school of Rural Domestic Economy was set up in the mansion house in the 1920s but only admitted girls! After the fire, a new building was erected near the site. The estate of Craibstone has a long and interesting history. It is thought that the land was gifted to a Flemish master gunner named John Crab as a reward for services to King Robert the Bruce at the Siege of Berwick in 1319. Up until that time, the land was known as Auchteronny but was later named after its owner, becoming Crabstoune in 1596 (from the Norse tun or enclosed land) then becoming Craibstone. The estate changed hands several times over the succeeding centuries being owned by Gordon of Abergeldie, three generations of the Sandilands family, Alexander Dauney and, in the early 19th century, it was bought by Alexander Scott whose family came from Huntly and who had made his fortune while in India. On his death, he instructed his trustees to provide an income from his land and investments to build and support Alexander Scott's Hospital in Gordon Road, Huntly. His legacy was to be used for the "aliment, clothing and lodging of old men and old women in the said town of Huntly". This hospital or home for the aged is still in existence, today housing 40 elderly people. After the death of Alexander's wife, Catherine Forbes of Boyndlie, the trustees rented out Craibstone House as a family home to the Davidson and Pirie families both of papermaking fame, successively.

The Green Burn had water drawn from it to the west of Craibstone estate into a mill lade that fed this water management system and mill dam. The burn powered several mills on its way to the River Don at Stoneywood. In 1865 and again in 1892/1905, the Ordnance Survey map of the area showed that the mill ground oats. In the middle of the 19th century, along with the rest of the Craibstone Estate, Alexander Scott, and later on his trustees, owned the farm and mill. However, by 1913, when it was taken over by the North College of Agriculture, the mill was said to be in poor condition and was to be replaced by an oil powered engine. Although the farmhouse and buildings of Mill of Craibstone are still in use, the mill has gone as has the mill dam. The area is now part of Scotland's Rural College campus.

Craibstone has always had a horticulture department teaching the growing of soft fruit, flowers and kitchen vegetables. From the early days, lecturers such as Mr. Moir and Mr. Panton visited local horticulture groups to talk about the work carried out at Craibstone and to answer questions. During the Second World War, Land Girls worked at Craibstone to help produce food when imported goods became almost non-existent. Beekeeping was also taught in the early days and one or two hives were kept at the gardens to fertilise the plants. Although the yield of honey was not great due to the need to disturb the hives for the students, the students benefited from the practical experience of apiary work.

Experimental plots were set up in a field at Craibstone in 1916 so that trials could be carried out on various soil types, different fertilizer treatments and plants. This would show how the plants progressed under diverse conditions and provide information for farmers and for students. It is said that when the plots were shown to some local farmers, they were dismissive because the plants were brairding (sprouting) unevenly. They did not accept that this was the point! In the early days, crops grown were cereals and root vegetables. Dairying, poultry rearing, veterinary health, agricultural engineering and forestry were also on the curriculum. After the First World War, injured soldiers and sailors were offered retraining in agriculture and forestry at Craibstone.

The Rowett Research Institute at Craibstone was first founded in 1913 by the North of Scotland College of Agriculture and Aberdeen University to study animal nutrition. John Boyd Orr – later Lord Boyd Orr was the first director of the college. He was instrumental in creating the laboratory block, insisting that it be built of granite rather than the intended cheaper wood. He was an eminent teacher, doctor, biologist and politician. During the First World War, he worked as a medical officer and was awarded the Military Cross and the Distinguished Service Order. In 1920 Boyd Orr approached John Quiller Rowett, a wealthy businessman who gave generously to the Institute at Craibstone. In recognition of his generosity, the Institute was named after him. Rowett made one condition - "if any work done at the Institute on animal nutrition were found to have a bearing on human nutrition, the Institute would be allowed to follow up this work." Over the years, The Rowett has been instrumental in many advances in both animal and human nutrition. In 2008, The Rowett became part of the University of Aberdeen.

This impressive house was built in 1850 and designed in the Jacobean style by James Matthews of Mackenzie and Matthews. It was commissioned by Alexander Pirie who owned Stoneywood Paper Mill. In 1851 he was living here with his wife, Charlotte, their four children and seven indoor servants. At that time, Alexander employed 193 men and 190 women.

Stoneywood Paper Mill looking to where the mill lade (centre) rejoins the River Don. Water power was crucial to the mill as it was the only natural power available in an area with no local coal. Between the First and Second World Wars, the River Don was frequently brightly coloured by the water emerging from the mills. This was stopped by the implementation of the Rivers (Prevention of Pollution) (Scotland) Act with its associated penalties. Of course, many rivers were polluted following the industrialisation of not only paper making but also mining and textile, chemical and metal manufacturing. Air pollution was also a problem with coal-fired boilers. Four chimneys are seen here and in 1899, the mills on the Don were said to 'belch forth columns of smoke'. However, the mills provided work for many and this mill was notable for looking after its workers with sport and social clubs, a school, a choir, and a brass band.

The entrance to Stoneywood Paper Mill was flanked by tall stone pillars with handsome finials. All the workers leaving the mill appear to be adults but this was not always so. In the early days, the mill employed children. However, the 1833 Factory Act stated that no children under 9 should be at work. There are reports of a boy of 12 being scalded when he fell into boiling liquid and of some children who had come off the night shift at Stoneywood getting into trouble on the Don when they lost the oars of a borrowed rowing boat. In 1878, the minimum age rose to 11 and by the early 1900s, it had risen to 12. The women are wearing boaters which were a popular fashion item in the late 19th to early 20th century and the men are wearing bunnets or caps. The coats worn by some of the women would indicate the first decade of the 20th century. Although these girls were mill workers, they were just as fashion conscious as more affluent women and would copy the styles of the day with cheaper materials.

Known locally as the Back Walk, this appears to be the tree-lined avenue that went from the main street opposite Market Street leading down towards Stoneywood Mill passing the Lodge to Stoneywood House on the left. This is now called Stoneywood Terrace. There is a large stone at the corner of the wall to prevent carts damaging the wall at this point. It is summer so the boys are barefoot as was common at the time. The girls in the distance are wearing typical Edwardian dresses and large hats.

The building on the centre right of the photograph was founded in 1864 by Messrs Pirie as a school for young workers in their mill at Stoneywood and also for the children of their adult workers. It was said to have been built in an 'elizabethan' style perhaps because of the gablets above the upper windows. The architect was James Matthews. The schoolrooms were in the single storey middle section with two storey schoolhouses at either end. The centre section was usually divided into two classrooms – one for girls and one for boys – but the partition could be removed to provide additional space when used as a hall. The bellcote is in the centre of the single storey. The building was later converted into a public hall where horticultural shows, weddings and scout gang shows were held. Although it can still be seen on Stoneywood Road, it has been extended and subdivided into dwelling houses. The entrance to Waterton House is on the left.

This scene shows Brimmond View, Stoneywood with the railway line running alongside, taken in the period after the houses were built but before the bungalows were erected between the First and Second World Wars. In 1927 a house on Brimmond View was advertised to let by the Aberdeen District Committee for £27 per annum. On the left can be seen setting out poles for the allotments that are still in use today. This land was part of Ruthriehill Farm and, from the drills, the farmer seems to be getting a last crop of tatties before the allotments take over. Ruthriehill was a mixed farm rearing pigs, poultry and cattle and growing potatoes and turnips. In 1867 Ruthriehill Farm was described as having a one storey farmhouse and steading slated and thatched and in good repair.

Persley Bridge on the River Don taking traffic from Mugiemoss Road over to Persley. Before the bridge was built there was a private ferry at this point. The bridge has five arches; three river arches and two land arches. As can be seen, there are cutwaters on the piers of the bridge. These strengthen the piers and, on the upstream side, help to deflect debris coming down the river. The Scatterburn enters the Don on the south bank just east of the bridge. A small settlement grew up on the slope from the Don up to around where Mugiemoss Road is today. On William Roy's map of 1747 – 1755, this settlement was called Hadagain (probably meaning a bend in a river) and the name has survived to this date in the infamous Haudagain Roundabout. An early name for the Scatter Burn was the Cruives Burn. Cruives were fixed salmon traps and gave their name to this area which used to be known as Old Cruives. In 1660, after some maintenance had been carried out on the cruives, the Earl of Mar and some other landowners in the upper reaches of the Don decided that the cruives were preventing too many salmon from reaching their stretches of river. Accordingly, they raised some 2,500 men and marched down to Persley. The local population decided against challenging them and Mar and his companions wrecked the cruives. They were subsequently rebuilt. It was decided to build the bridge in 1888 but due to obstructive tactics by Alexander Pirie, of the Stoneywood Paper Works, the work was not completed until 1892 after Aberdeen Council paid Pirie to remove his objection. The council also part funded the bridge. At a bend in the river just east of this point is Snuffies Pool – a favourite haunt of salmon poachers in years gone by. It would seem that the pool got its name from the nickname given to the owner of the snuff mill that used to stand just below Persley Castle. The mill was originally built as a waulk or fulling mill, then converted into a copper mill around 1752. Shortly after that, it became a snuff mill.

Lower Persley Quarry was leased by George Hall Building Contractors and Granite Merchants from the first decade of the 1900s. In this photograph a skip slung from a Blondin is used to carry blocks of granite. Granite quarried here was light grey in colour and was suitable for building or the making of granite setts for roads but it would not take a polish so it could not be used for decorative work. George Hall ceased trading in the early 1960s but the quarry was closed some years before that. Stone from this quarry was used to build the railway viaduct over the River Dee in Aberdeen and also the Teacher Training College. In 1923 George Hall won the contract both for the supply of granite and for the construction of the War Memorial Court, the Art Gallery Extension and the Art Museum in Aberdeen.

Charles Davidson was born at Farburn in Newhills Parish in 1772 and was reputed to be descended from the Davidsons of Tarland. He trained as a millwright at Grandholm Waulk Mill on the Don before going into partnership with Charles Smith of Stoneywood Mill. The partnership was short-lived and Charles went back to work at Grandholm. In 1811 Charles obtained a 57 year lease for some land and buildings at Mugiemoss upstream of the junction of the Bucks Burn and the River Don. On the land there was an old mill lade that had fed water-powered mills but was disused. Mills for various purposes had existed at this site for many years. Charles set up a waulk mill (a mill for fulling cloth) and a snuff mill at the junction of the Bucks Burn and the River Don. Probably around 1821, Charles began to manufacture paper. Although he set up the business, it was his sons, William and George Davidson who expanded it after they inherited their father's half of the business on his death in 1843. However, a devastating fire in 1853 meant that they had to rebuild the whole mill and took the opportunity to expand and update the works. By the 1870s Mugiemoss Paper Mill was reputed to be the largest producer of paper bags in Britain. Later, they were also producing plasterboard liner, wrapping paper, boxboards and refuse sacks. In 2005, the mill closed with the loss of nearly 300 jobs.

Mugie Moss Paper Works, Auchmill,
Aberdeenshire, 29th Sept., 1888.

Archibald Duff Esq
Aberdeen

C. DAVIDSON & SONS, LIMITED.

Enclosed I beg to send you Warrant for Dividend —less Income Tax—on your Shares in this Company, as declared at the Annual General Meeting, on 26th inst., as follows :—

330 Old Shares (£1 paid up), at 1/3 per Share,	£	20 : 12 : 6
120 New Shares (10/- paid up), at 7½d. do.		4 : 1 : 3
		24 : 13 : 9
Less Income Tax,		11 : 4
	£	24 : 2 : 5

WILLIAM MILNE,
Secretary.

A Muggie Moss Paper Works share notice of 1888 showing a dividend of £24:2:3 (with income tax deducted). Meanwhile, paper mill workers on the Don were working over 70 hours a week with one Saturday off a fortnight – after coming off night shift. For this, they earned between 14 shillings and 27 shillings a week depending on skill level. At this time butter was 1 shilling a pound, bacon 9d, cheese 4d and bogey roll pipe tobacco was 6d for 2 oz. However, tobacco was probably a rare treat.

In 1886, a group of employees of Mugiemoss Paper Mill formed a football club – reported to be the oldest junior club in the north of Scotland. Over the years, they won many honours as can be seen from the array of cups in the photograph. By 1947 they had been League Champions of the Aberdeen Junior Football Association thirteen times and gained many other local awards. The success of the club resulted in some players going on to play professional football for Aberdeen, Clyde, Motherwell, Dundee United, Leeds United and Glasgow Rangers. A number of players represented Scotland at junior level. The most successful team for the club was that of 1909-1910 and although this photograph is not dated, it may celebrate that team. Rosslyn Sport FC had been founded in 1923 and when both clubs got into difficulty over their home grounds, the two clubs merged to found Dyce Juniors in 1989. The Mugiemoss colours of black and white stripes are still used as Dyce Sport FC's away strip.

Persley Den appears to be a beautiful work of nature but in fact, it is entirely man-made. The River Don has powered many mills over the years and Persley Den was dug as a mill lade to take water to the mills at Grandholm. The earliest record of a mill at Grandholm downstream of Persley is in the 1790s when it was used to spin flax. Leys & Co employed men to dig this mill lade to take water from the River Don to power the works at Grandholm. It is more than a mile long and had to be diverted round a hill and in places rock had to be removed to a depth of 20ft in order to maintain the necessary gradient. It is reported that this work took hundreds of men several years. This mill lade and its surrounding banks are now Persley Den. In 1826, Leys commissioned Hewes and Wren of Manchester to build a water wheel for the works. It was said to be the largest in the world at 25 feet diameter and weighing 100 tons. The wheel is now housed in a museum in Edinburgh.

Persley Den was a popular spot for picnics. Families from Aberdeen would take the tram to Woodside Fountain and then walk down a steep flight of 66 steps known as Jacob's Ladder to the Don. The steps took them to a private bridge for workers at Grandholm Textile Mills but it could also be used by the general public. From there, a path led to the Den. They could also take the Suburban Train (the subbie) to Persley Halt. Families from Bucksburn would walk down Goodhope Brae to Mugiemoss Road, crossing the Don by Persley Bridge. I believe it was a great place to collect rasps.